Rita Baki

is a writer and an emotional intelligence coach living
between Dubai and Beirut. She is a teacher, a healer,
and a mother of two. Her life is devoted to helping people
connect with their truth and empowering them to live
a fulfilled life. Her story follows a woman's path
to self-realization:
"Torn between two worlds, tradition and freedom,
I was confused between my roles as a mother and wife
and manager, yet beneath it all a teenager longing for a wild
free life and love. I challenged societal norms, marriages,
and tradition - all for freedom of choice...
When we learn how our mind works, and understand
that we can heal through different energies and states
of consciousness, we have the ability to change every
single aspect of our lives."

honeysuckle

your journal. yours.
spirited by —— R i t a B a k i

AUSTIN MACAULEY PUBLISHERS™
LONDON • CAMBRIDGE • NEW YORK • SHARJAH

ISBN – 9789948769880 – (Paperback)
ISBN – 9789948769873 – (E-Book)

Application Number: MC-10-01-3875835
Age Classification: E

Printer Name: iPrint Global Ltd
Printer Address: Witchford, England

First Published 2024
AUSTIN MACAULEY PUBLISHERS FZE
Sharjah Publishing City
P.O. Box [519201]
Sharjah, UAE
www.austinmacauley.ae
+971 655 95 202

This journal is dedicated to my children.
Sarah and Nadim, thank you for being my reason
to stay and write.

Honeysuckle; *genus Lonicera;*

any of 180 plants of this family;
these climbers flourish in almost any type of soil; reaching up,
twisting, covering, blooming with white, yellow, orange, red,
purple, or scarlet flowers;
sprouting black, red, or orange berry fruit;
covering fields, gardens, and homes in blankets of sweet fragrance;
calling insects, bees, and
hummingbirds to play;

*dancing with nature
and life all at once.*

Writing Journal
& Instructions

This journal is a ritual.
It is an invitation to face the truth,
to let the hurt out, scream it into words,
and let it land on these pages.
The prompts here flow from my spirit
to meet yours;
use them to reclaim all the lost pieces
of your being.

*Beloved one, write. Write it all out, in any alphabet,
in any language, in any form that comes from
your magnificent heart, for this is where the healing is.*

May the strength, resilience,
sweetness, and beauty
of the wild honeysuckle

find you here.

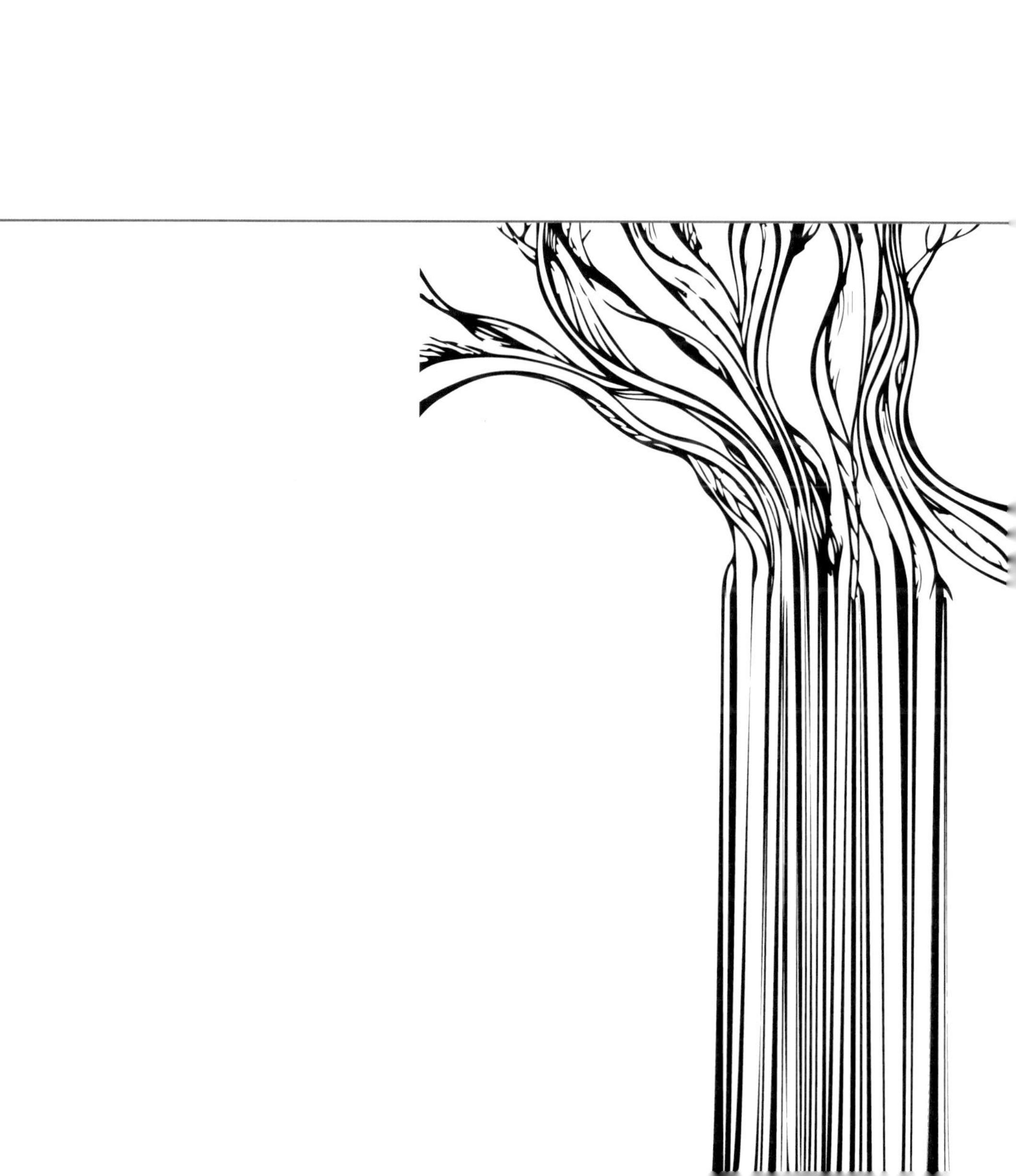

Unwind.

She is fierce, yet soft, a fine-looking gypsy, a rebel inside-out.
She smells of love and peace and Chanel sometimes,
her favorite perfume, Chanel No 5.

No. 19 at times for the smoky, musky, mystery that she is.
She speaks of poetry, lyrics, the mind and the heart;
she is a well of an old soul.
Brown eyes, you are my everything, "healthy wild drive"
she was once told.

Truth is her tongue, listens well and can pick up pieces and
turn them into delicate patch work. She has patched a once
broken master piece, herself and others; that's what she does for
a living, patch work of master pieces called humans.
All she wants is to live a full life... whatever full is to her.

The pen, the keyboard, music, coffee, horses, the desert, and the
sun are what she breathes in to breathe out love.
White, white is her favorite color, goes well with the tan.
The tan is a must, it's part of her skin. The sun kisses need to be
visible all year round. She wears a bronzing crème when she is
not tanned, she insists on the tan.

Winter is not her cup of tea, she can take it for few days
to cuddle but the sun, the sun is her oxygen.
Few best friends, all love cuddles and hugs and are loved
equally, madly.

Favorite food is Indian, must have picked it from a past life.
Childhood: that's a tough one. Love, love, and love is needed,
didn't get much of it.

Childhood memories are not so pleasant,
at least the ones she recalls.
First memory, not important at this stage.
She makes memories now, memories in the making.
She might have shut off some memories…it's possible…
but that's a choice or a vow, yes, a vow to start all over again, to
close tight windows and doors of history.

Favorite shoes are slippers, they show the details of the toes
that have walked miles and miles of pain and sorrow and fun,
they tell so much, you will be surprised at how much agony
those groomed toe nails have witnessed and heard
and turned direction.

High heels at times, worn like masks.
Favorite song is Annie's song of John Denver.
The lyrics go:

*You fill up my senses, like a night in a forest, Like the
mountains in springtime, like a walk in the rain, Like a storm
in the desert, like a sleepy blue ocean…You fill up my senses,
come fill me again…*

Mia, it is Mia, that's all she is. Mia, as in the movie Mamma-Mia

*Here we go again…my, my how can I resist you…I've been
cheated by you since I don't know when So I made up my
mind, it must come to an end…*

She looks like a rider, a woman of horses, tamed horses.
When she stands in front of a full length mirror, she sees:
womanhood, motherhood, love, pride, beauty, success,
all personified in one figure.
And sometimes she sees lumps and bumps and wishes they
were not there.
And sometimes she sees broken glass on the mirror.
And sometimes she doesn't see through.
And sometimes the figure speaks back to her and says you are
beautiful just the way you are, just the way you are.
And sometimes she believes and sometime she doesn't.
And sometimes she answers and sometimes she ignores.
And sometimes she sees other people in the reflection clung
on all parts of her body.
And sometimes she smells freedom.
And sometimes the image is dark.
And sometimes the image is light.
And sometimes heavy.
And sometimes warm.
And sometimes a mirage.
But all the time it's her, the one and only Mia.

She is neither skinny nor chubby, light, fine, medium length
chestnut hair, always-groomed nails, nose pierced, a gold stud
inserted snugly in the crease.

Long skirts, hippie dresses, and head wraps
are her favorite outfit.

Rudraksha necklace around her neck, always.
Ivory teeth, thick bushy eye brows, the white in her eyes is blue.
Bruised knees, from the amount of falls
she has had as a child and adult.

Birth mark on the inner knee like a bread loaf, as if bread was
forbidden even before she was born.

Curves, she's full of curves.

Glossy or red lips, never a third color.
Nude, red, or black are the three colors of her manicure,
never a fourth, consistency helps.

She craves salty food, sweets are not her favorite.

1

If you were the main character in a movie, who would you be?

Describe yourself, all of yourself.

2

Some days, all I want to do is write, lay down, and cuddle with my characters.

List all the characters in your story, how do you feel about them?

3

Every day, I remember, write, and feel the
pain; feel the pain, write, and remember;
and sometimes, write, feel the pain,
and remember.

What remembrance is calling you today?
Invite it here and write together.

4

**I'm still tripping on your shadows.
Inner work.**

*Our shadow self is a part of us
that we reject or refuse to see.
It often lives in a bag on our shoulders.
Let your shadows out of their hiding place
and onto these pages.*

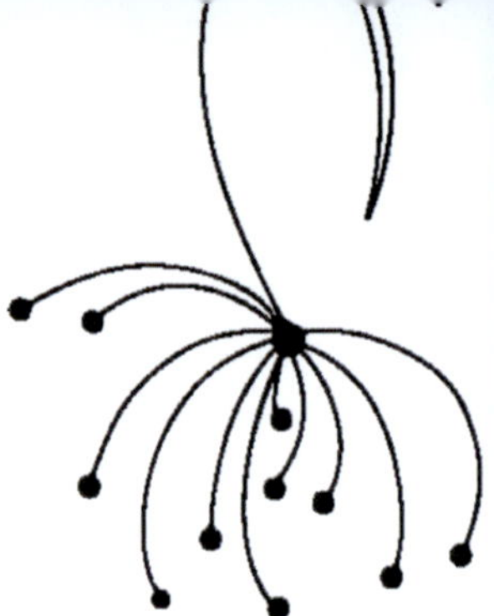

5

A Poem for life in the Lebanon

Lives hanging
Aunt on breathing machine
Grey faces
Dry eyes
Mom on a coat's edge
Cats waiting to be fed
Cracks in ceilings
Rain dripping through
Fire keepers by night
Snow at 1400 m above sea level
Protests at sea level and beyond
Observers we have become
"Feed the poor" Sunday declared
Young men's lives ending in a breeze
Frozen blood on wrinkled faces
A glimpse. A moan. A curse.
Survive on a dash of myrrh
A divorcee sunk in folklore and graffiti
Sons, grandsons
I-d-entity
Courage
Questions
Awaiting answers
Salt in corners
Ash under skin
A frame of a golden sun
A Mediterranean winter on ancestral earth
Whispers of the hearts
Hymns of the souls
United
We survive
Beirut-Dec-2019.

For the love of lists, let them flow.
What's on your list today?

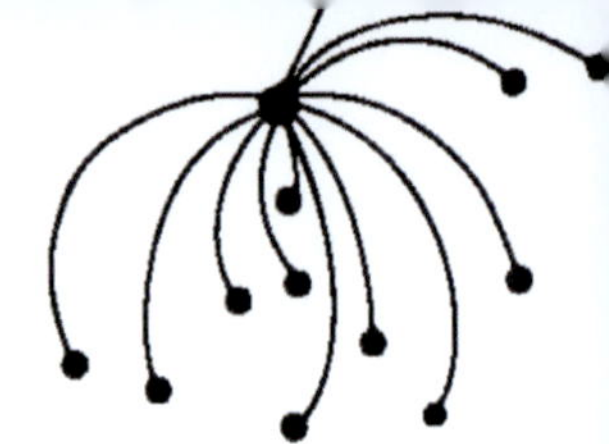

6

At bedtime
I tucked her in,
Under layers and layers of memories,
Years of hiding.
One night she came out and said
I don't feel safe, I never felt safe.
And I then realized,
tucking her in was never enough.
My inner child.

Return to your inner child.
What does it need most from you today?

7

The name that was music to my ears,
becomes the pain of the years,
becomes the beat that drums 'depart'
on that fine muscle of the heart.

Whose name is it?

And I became a graveyard
of all the lives buried within
An altar for the dead
Come, light a candle at my feet.
Beirut.

When your favorite city speaks,
what does she say to you?

9

Coexistence:
Tell me how, how places become people
and people become places?
And the only place in your heart
you want them to fill, they deny.
They cannot co-exist.

Who is denying you space?

10

I miss you to an extent, that I want
to do nothing but close my eyes and savor
the flavors of all the times I was with you,
one mouthful at a time.
Craving you.

Who do you miss most?

11

I died twice
The day we met and the day you left us.
Today I went to my drawers,
Fetched everything you got me,
And wanted to wear them all
The labyrinth necklace,
The blue stone pendant,
The bracelets,
Then I drank your favorite tea in your mug
And savored on scented paper
and your notepad
Maybe, just maybe…
I hear your voice through the stones
Or see your face through the tea.
Today, my heart mourns you,
As I celebrate your life.
God knows, the struggle is real
To mourn and celebrate
To grief and rejoice
To love you and say goodbye
To hold you and let you go
Rest my love
Rest with the stars
Rest with the moon and the music
We will forever love you.
Joanna.

This space is for your grief.

12

Ever felt like your voice doesn't travel
Your words, your breath, your gaze, your spirit.
They all just don't travel.
Frozen.

What part of you is stagnant today?
Breathe into it,
allow it to express itself,
let it move once more…

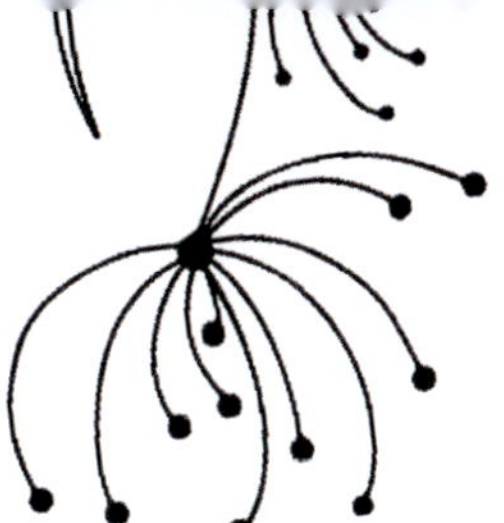

Choking on Flames:
My twin.

What are you choking on?
Cough it out in letters.

14

Rage, sadness, love, bitterness, passion,
success, happiness,
All made it to the finish line.
It's the kind of victory that is neither
celebrated nor mourned,
It is buried.

What are you bringing closure to today?

15

That piece of you, I carry inside of me, is heavy.

Let go of something on these pages.

16

I accepted the 'nothing' offered
I stayed,
I looked for love outside me, in you
And you gave me all you had of love, nothing.
You gave me your all of "nothing" and
I received it all
It occupied so much space in me
Nothing left of me but the nothing of you.
Searching for me in piles of nothingness.

*Here's to more lessons of love,
self-worth and worth of heart.*

Unfold.

1

And what if you write of sunsets?
What if you read of desert sands?
What if you speak the hearts?
What if you listen?
What if you truly feel?
Is that more resolution than you can handle?

Make a vow here.

2

You wake up one day and look at your daughter
and say, this is the woman I raised,
and she is the sum of all the women
who lived within.
Revelations

What is your revelation?

3

Flow:
Lack of,
Hurts.

*What is being lost in the repetition
and routines that sneak into our lives?
Birth a new rhythm today.*

4

The medicine man.
"Gaze at the organic," he said
The clouds, the sand grains,
The waves,
The mother's intelligence,
The Divine magnificence.
I listened and gazed beyond the clouds,
the grains and waves to find a lost song
in the graves,
a lost voice longing to respond.
I awake, to save me, and we bond.

*This space is for your conversation
with mother nature.*

5

Are you betraying them with me
or betraying me with them?
Am I betraying myself with you
Or myself is betraying me?
Am I writing those words
Or those words are writing me?
Am I loving life
Or life is loving me
By bringing you to me
And taking me from you?

Let there be trust now. I trust...

6

The wasabi, the flu or I just miss you?
I nibble on Sushi, maki and lots of wasabi
My companion, the flu.
An entourage of cough and tears queue.
Is it the flu, the wasabi or I just miss you?

Let the tears out.

7

I don't talk about you
But they see you in my eyes
And feel you in my breath
And hear you in my heartbeats
And smell you in my hair
They sense you are under my skin
And I wonder, how much more they know?
And how much more I show?
I don't utter a word
Yet my lips
My lips speak silently
And everybody seems to understand
The secret language of my lips
I can't hide you anymore
I let my throat loose and confessed
you to the skies.

Who are you confessing to?

8

Watch with me,
The light forgetting the darkness.
Mornings

Time to pause.

9

Rid me of it all
It: The pain
Take me to the skies
where the clouds kiss the rain
And send them messengers to my heart:
the raindrops.

Create with the letters of your name.

10

**Silence treatments do not work
on this side of the heart.**

*What is being lost in the silence?
Here, let no words go unsaid.*

11

It took me forever to undo the tangles and sleep again.

What keeps you up at night?

12

Skin will fall out
Other parts will tumble in your own hands too
Spit them out
Un-swallow your tongue
Dust all the carpets
Revive all the deaths you denied
Drink all the love
Sneeze all the fog
Cup all the rotten blood
It will bruise but soon clear
Let it begin
A life, within a life, within a life.
1001 lives.

I Allow…

13

You never loved me.
You loved the idea of me molding
into something,
Something you'll love.
When I stopped becoming that,
You left.

Disappointment, write about that.

I lay in bed, drowning in the loneliness of solitude, before I give birth to life beyond his aftershave.

What are you birthing?

15

Little did I know, that when they leave
they take pieces of you with them.
And it takes time to heal.
God knows it takes time.

Are you giving it time?

Unchain.

1

**I found more happiness in you
than you can find in happiness itself.**

What brings happiness to your heart?

2

For I am Not in pain.
More in fear,
Of the Unknown
How it unfolds
What it damages
What it heals
What it takes
What it leaves
Will there be scars?
Will they hurt?

This space is for your biggest fears.

3

I'd tell you a thousand times I love you
But some love is better experienced
than confessed
Your love is better savored than discussed.
Sincerely…my love

How do you express love?

4

Things I'd tell / ask you
but I won't…
I'd tell you, "Last Christmas I gave you my heart,"
but I won't
I'd tell you, "This year, I'm hiding from you
and your soul of ice,"
but I won't
I'd ask you, "Tell me we had something…"
but I won't
I'd ask you, "Did you call them all the same
names you call me?
Did they respond as I do? Are they as true?"
but I won't
I'd tell you, "I envy the names you call,"
but I won't
I'd tell you, "You marked your territory over
my dead body,"
but I won't
I'd ask you, "If my perfume traumatizes you
as yours does to me…"
but I won't
I'd ask you, "Do you think of me as much
as I do of you?"
but I won't
I'd tell you, "You add life to my life,"
but I won't
I won't ask, because I know all the answers
I'd tell you all the answers,
but I won't
There's no point
This Christmas I save me from tears.
Detach, move on woman.

*What can you do today to detach
and move one baby step forward?*

5

I am sorry
My babies,
For all the times life got in the way
of expressing how much I love you
For all the times I missed your growth
For all the times I didn't say enough of what
you sought
For all the times I could have loved you
more than I thought
For all the times I was busy growing up
with you
For all the times I failed you
For all the times your heart spoke
and my ears didn't listen
and my mouth didn't talk
For all the times… I am sorry
I hold you in my heart-cage forever
I surrender my breath to save yours
For I will live through you
Go on, explore, enjoy life, grow beyond,
take my mistakes as your learnings,
be better, and teach me more…
Take my love and love even more…
Mom

Who needs to hear your "sorry"?
The time is now.

6

When my carpet speaks:
I am a colorful Persian carpet,
I feel stepped on, ignored, admired less,
worthless.
I'd rather be treated gently, lovingly,
I have roots but no true connection,
I talk to the windows and
allow the rays to caress my limbs,
I dream of traveling with you
to your future beach house,
I dream of witnessing your lover's intimacy
at my feet.
What worries me is stagnation
and drop in value.
I would like the world to think of me
as precious, beautiful, and lovable as I am.
What keeps me awake is your loneliness
and your confusion.
The best thing I have done
is keeping you warm when it gets cold.
The worst thing I have ever done is wrinkle
and trip them as they cross over you.
I feel guilty for being so static.
My favorite time of the night
is when I am tucked in,

And it's so quiet,
and I help you find your lines to spill.
The point of my life is to keep
you warm and inspired.
I would like to be remembered
as a loud piece of art.

*Choose one of your belongings
and allow it to speak to and through you.*

7

I needed to wake up to the rays
and take my feet to the sand
I needed to talk to the waters and taste the
salt
I needed to feel my tongue
I needed to ask all the questions
Maybe, just maybe, if I hear the answers
in a different language
I'll believe them.
Denial.

What truth are you not accepting?

8

I smelled them
The showered,
The non-showered,
The depressed,
The euphoric,
The joints,
The perfumed,
The body smells,
The cheap creams,
The coffee blends,
The za'atar,
The fish,
The bait,
The fishermen,
The deserted boats,
The mosque,
The men swimming in boxers.
All walking this morning towards something,
away from something,
for someone…maybe.
Beirut walks in the morning.

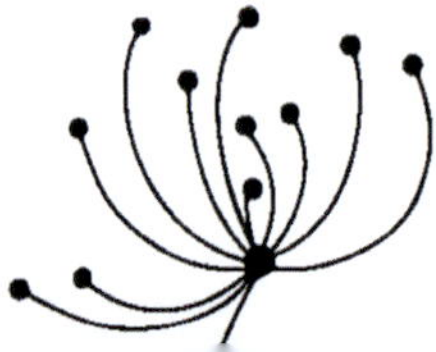

*Journey into nature
and write.*

9

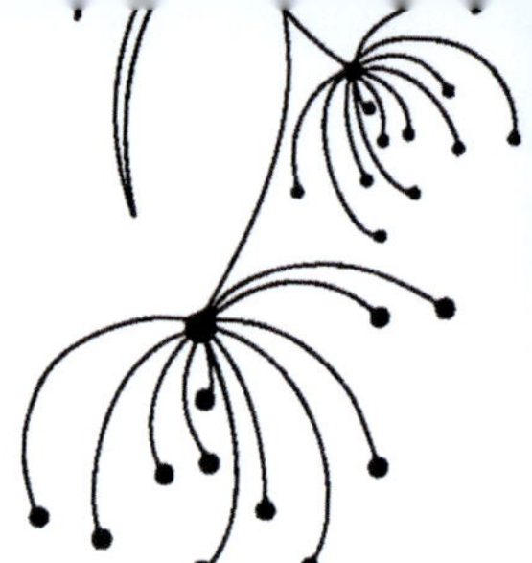

Walls have ears
Let them listen
Let them watch
Let them take notes
Let them witness
Let them learn
How it's done
The harmony
The flow

What are your walls listening to?

10

Mama
When I'm old, and I look at you with empty eyes
Know that I still love you
When I ask you 190 times the same question
Answer me with love
Soon you will wish I kept asking
and not gone into silence
When I disconnect
Love me
When I choke because I forgot to swallow
my own saliva
Love me
Make my favorite food, I won't ask for it
And when I eat and make a mess
Ignore the mess and love me
When I scream in pain all night
Love me, for I am soul-searching
Help me stay neat and beautiful,
brush my hair and my
eyebrows, fix my nails and steam my clothes,
I want to leave as I came, beautiful
When I go, let me go in peace
For I miss the lightness of being.

*Connect to an old soul today
and write.*

11

They hide in coffee
And sneak into journals,
Uninvited at times.

Who hides in your coffee cups?

12

Today at the beach,
Someone was wearing your perfume,
I died and incarnated,
A little girl on your lap,
Understanding life through your smell.

*See the world through the eyes
of someone who loves you,
what is it saying?*

13

**My heart is feeling more than life should allow
It was something in his being holding
the same longing.**

What / who gives you life?

14

Tonight I put on my favorite,
Black, sadness outfit
Sophisticated, refined accessories knit,
Weaved over my heart, perfect fit
Fancy, heavy shoulder wrap
Glittering chains,
dripping from my neck to my lap
Party shoes, perfect to tap…
DANCE
Each move rattles with chains
Each tap battles with reigns
I undress to the core,
The outfit and all
Naked on the dance floor
NOW DANCE.

DANCE

15

I used to worry, now I just write.

Just Write